Contemporary Traditions in Native American Jewelry

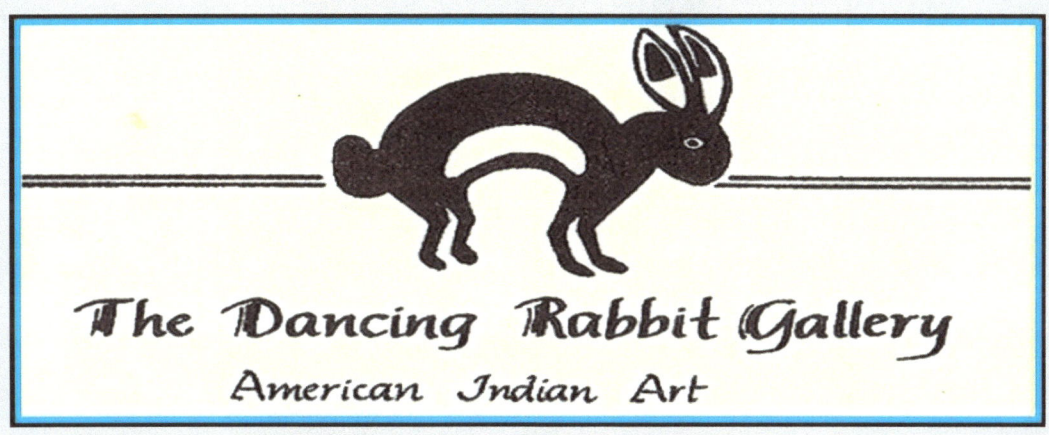

Katie McClain Richarme
Michael Richarme, Ph.D.

Contemporary Traditions in Native American Jewelry

The second book in this series examines the evolution of traditional Native American jewelry into contemporary forms and designs.

Jewelry tells a story of culture, and Native American artists look to tell their cultural stories with historic designs interwoven into the modern world.

This book focuses on new trends in design and the use of gemstones highlighting several Native American artists who are at the forefront of this evolution.

Art always pushes the envelope = art always evolves.

Evolution

The origins of jewelry are shrouded in the mists of time, but we can certainly speculate. Used for worship, adornment, and counting wealth, jewelry likely started as shiny or irregularly shaped objects found by people as they went about their daily lives. These objects may have been stones with bright colors, or representations of aspects of the world in which they lived, but they gained intrinsic meaning above and beyond the material aspect of the actual stone.

Artistic inspiration often derives from an interpretation of the natural world, with the artist forming a mental image of the work before they even begin. Technical expertise, sets of skills learned through generations of trial and error and passed down through family members, is required to carefully and precisely manipulate the materials to bring the mental picture to fruition.

Turquoise

Turquoise has been utilized by Native Americans for a long time, as the gem is widely found in the American Southwest.

It is a soft gemstone, and often includes a lot of crumbly chalk materials when mined from the ground. When purchasing turquoise, buyers should always question whether the stone is natural or stabilized (coated in a transparent material to prevent erosion of the soft turquoise stone, and possibly prevent discoloration).

It is hard to know exactly the mine from which the turquoise was extracted, as even within a single mine, the matrix of turquoise and substrate materials like copper may vary. But some mines have strong tendencies, like Sleeping Beauty or Number 8, and experts can recognize the likelihood that a specific mine produced a specific stone.

The relatively unknown Skyline Turquoise Mine is in Lander County, Nevada. Each of these exquisite natural turquoise stones is hand cut by the artist. The range of colors provides the most beautiful deep shades of turquoise, blue and green.

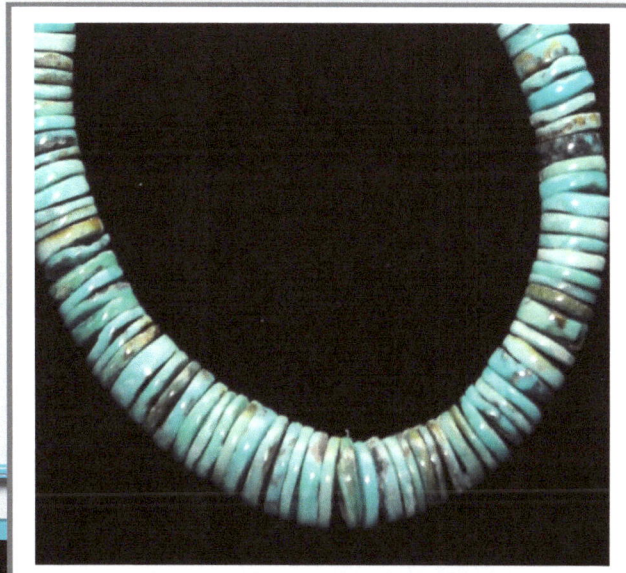

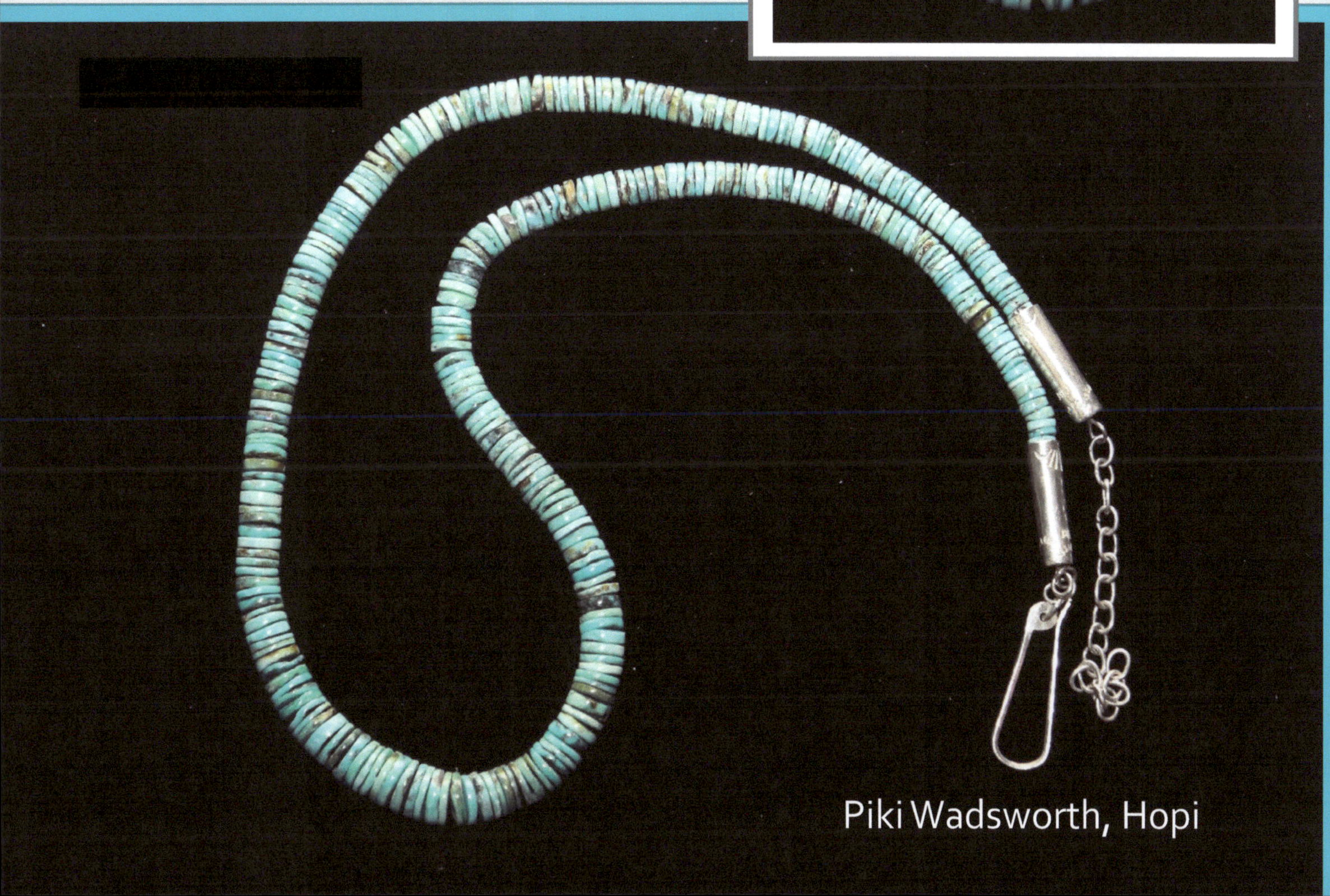

Piki Wadsworth, Hopi

These exquisite stones are natural Candelaria Turquoise. Candelaria turquoise deposits produced quality stones in shades of light sea blue to rich dark blue with varying colors of webbing. Today Candelaria turquoise is very rare and seldom seen. It is considered highly desirable.

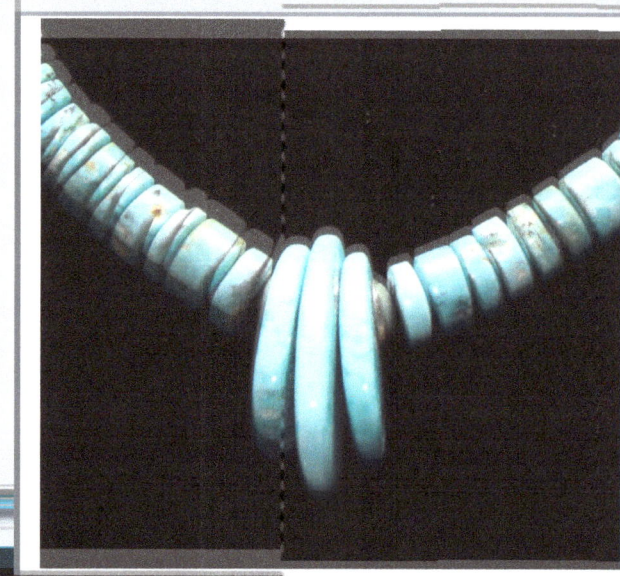

Piki Wadsworth, Hopi

The Morenci turquoise in this ring and cuff is of the highest gem quality. Albert set each of the stones in both the ring and cuff in sterling silver with 14k gold accents and bezels on each side.

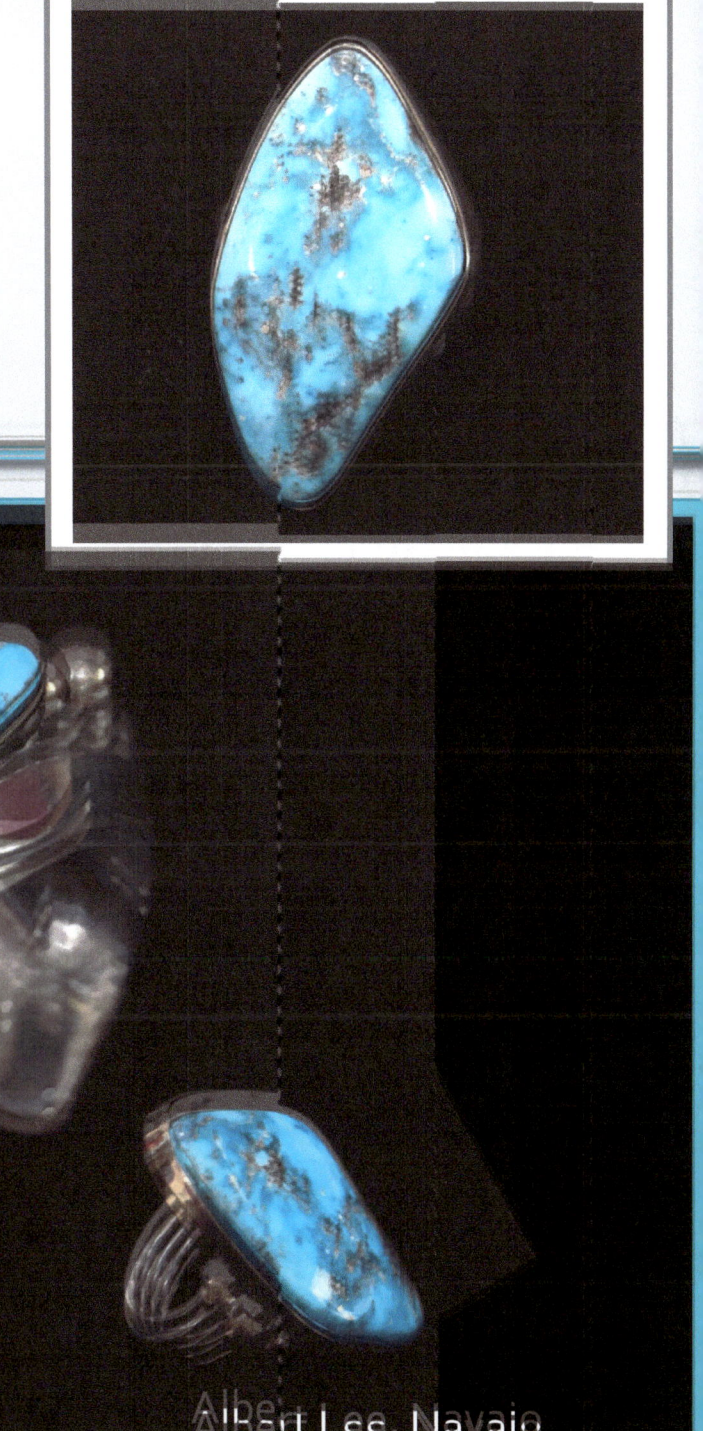

Albert Lee, Navajo

Green Turquoise

Although becoming scarce, green turquoise from Nevada has been popular among collectors for generations. The bold vivid color variations of lime green, emerald green, and military green are unique to Nevada. Green turquoise can be found in the same mine alongside blue turquoise; it just depends on the chemical composition at the time of the stone formation.

Three of the more famous mines producing beautiful green turquoise are the Royston Turquoise mine, the Ciraco Lake mine, and the Northern Lights mine.

Due to the rarity of natural green turquoise, many contemporary artists are using Gaspeite in their jewelry. Gaspeite is a rare mineral resembling green turquoise in appearance. It forms in a variety of shades of green, from very light apple green to a much darker shade and contains a brown matrix.

Varying shades of green in the turquoise and in the gaspeite showcase the colors of these beautiful minerals.

The cuff is Royston turquoise; the ring is Ciraco Lake turquoise and the inset cuff is Northern Lights turquoise. The necklace is Gaspeite by an unknown artist.

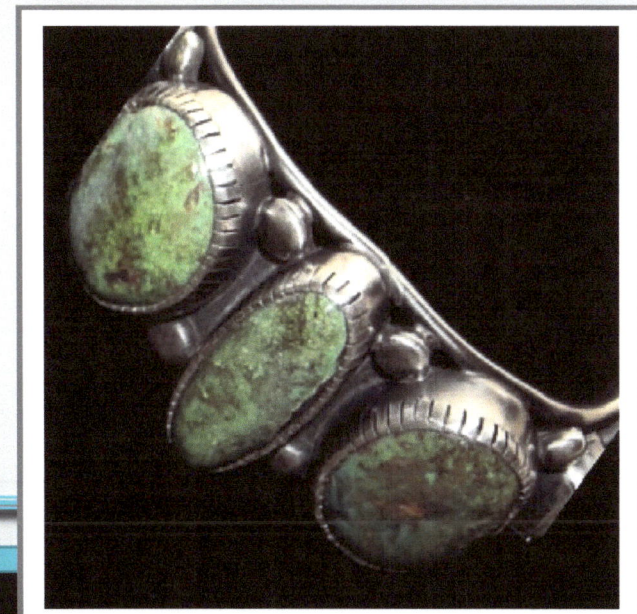

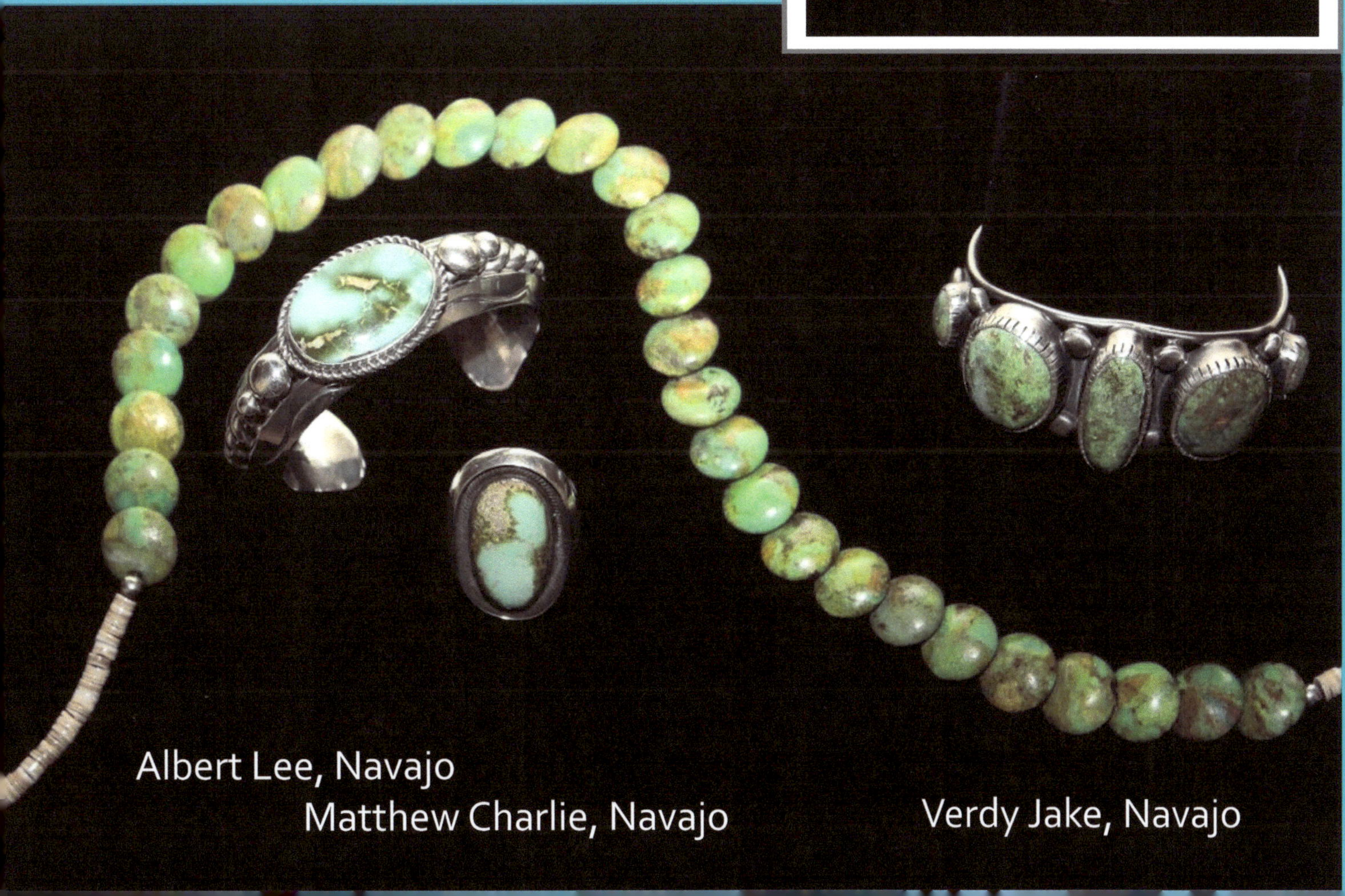

Albert Lee, Navajo
Matthew Charlie, Navajo
Verdy Jake, Navajo

Gold

Man has had a fascination with gold for many millennia, and it is highly sought as a base material for elegant jewelry.

The warmth of the color creates a platform for almost any design or stone, and the tensile strength of gold in its different karats allows the artists to work the materials into intricate molds and shapes.

Gold stays pure in its chemical composition, and does not react to skin oils or moderate wear.

Natural Kingman spider web turquoise is quite rare, making up only one percent of product mined at the Kingman Mine. Piki accents the undulating colors of this rare turquoise with 18k gold accent beads.

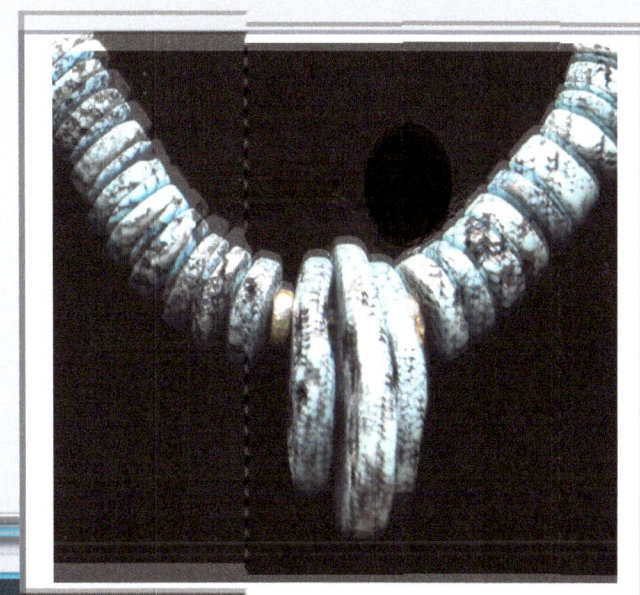

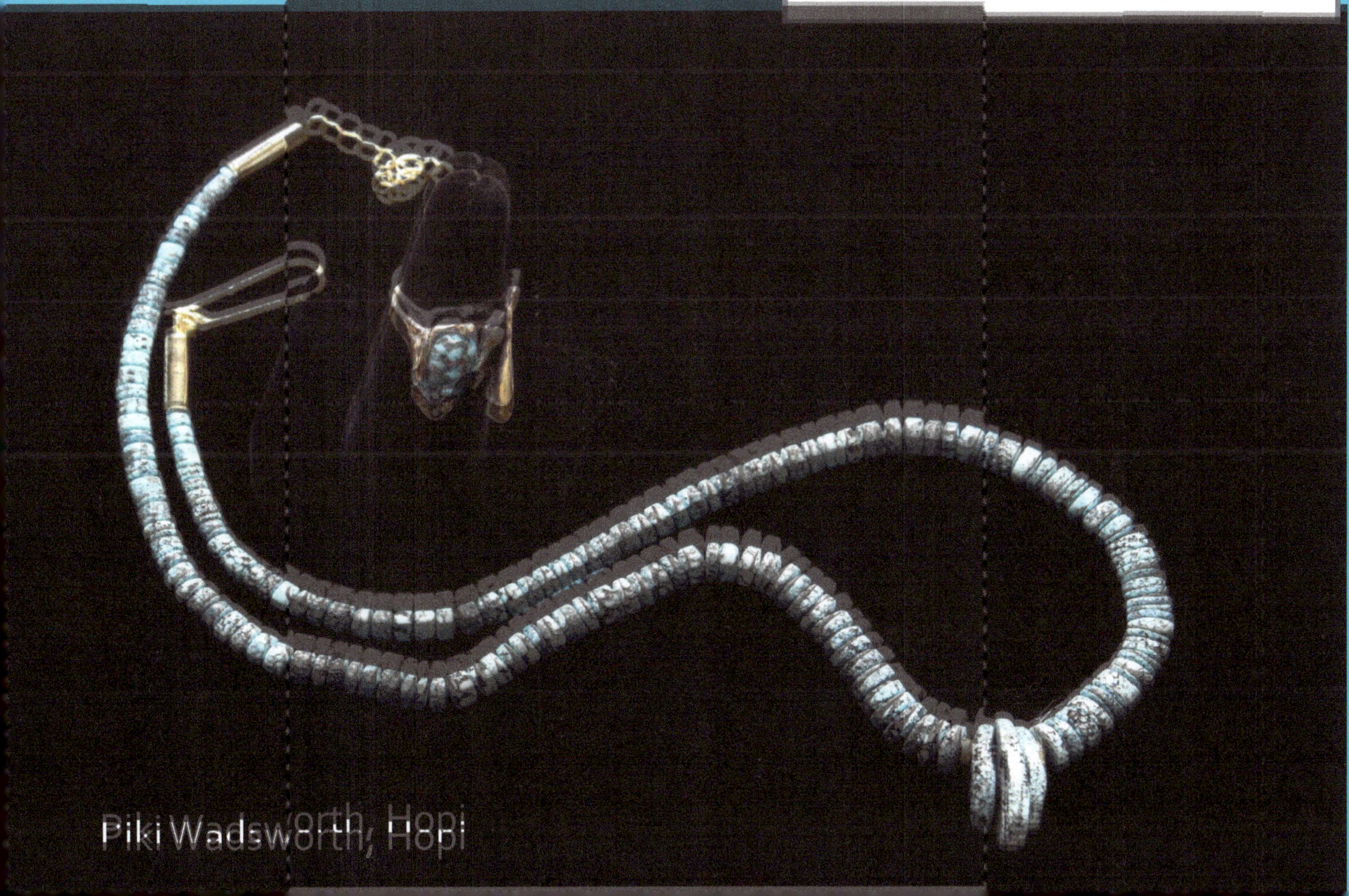

Piki Wadsworth, Hopi

This incredible cuff of 18k gold has been cast in tufa stone. Steve then placed 105 Australian fire opals individually in perfectly raised bezels to highlight the deep fire of each stone. The beautiful design of the fiery hued opals evokes the look of corn which is vital to the Hopi.

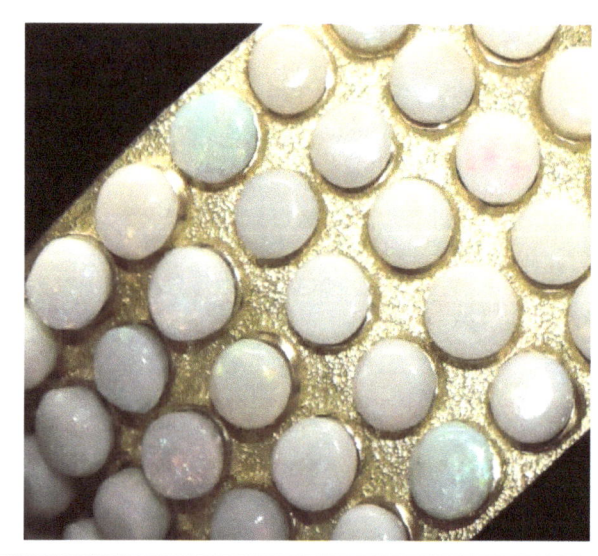

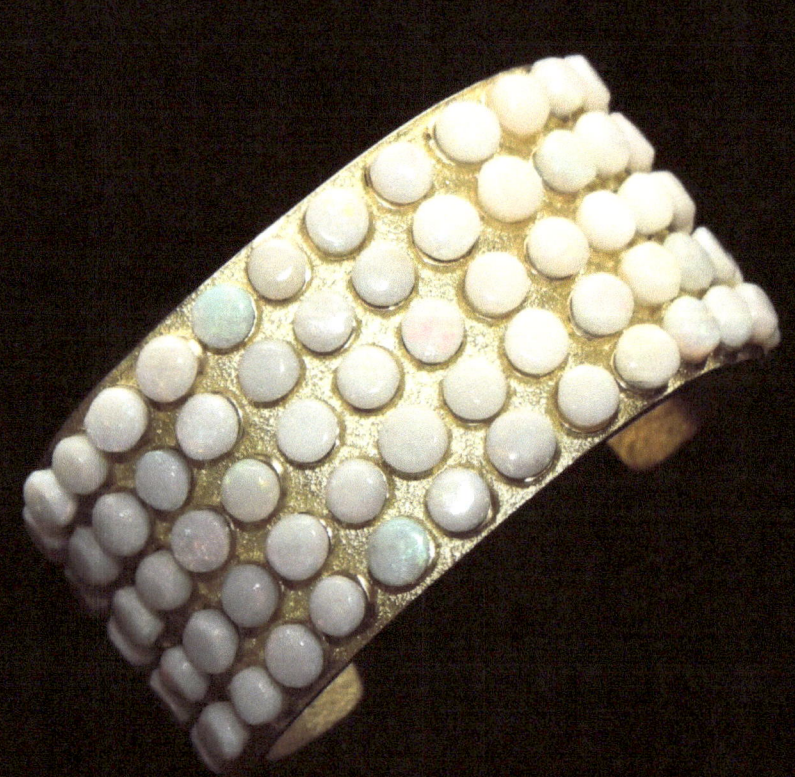

Steve LaRance, Hopi

Inlaid with natural Blue Gem turquoise, gold and natural Australian opal, this starburst pendant by Michael Kirk shimmers in the light. The iridescence of the opals emphasizes the slivers of 14K gold in earrings by Thomas Barbre.

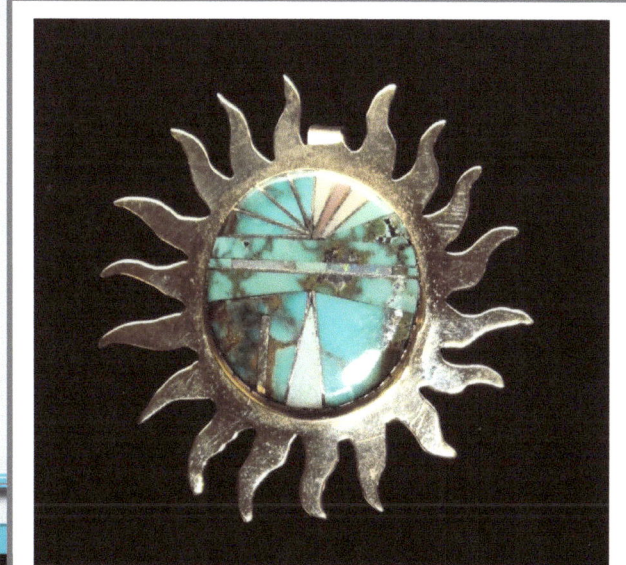

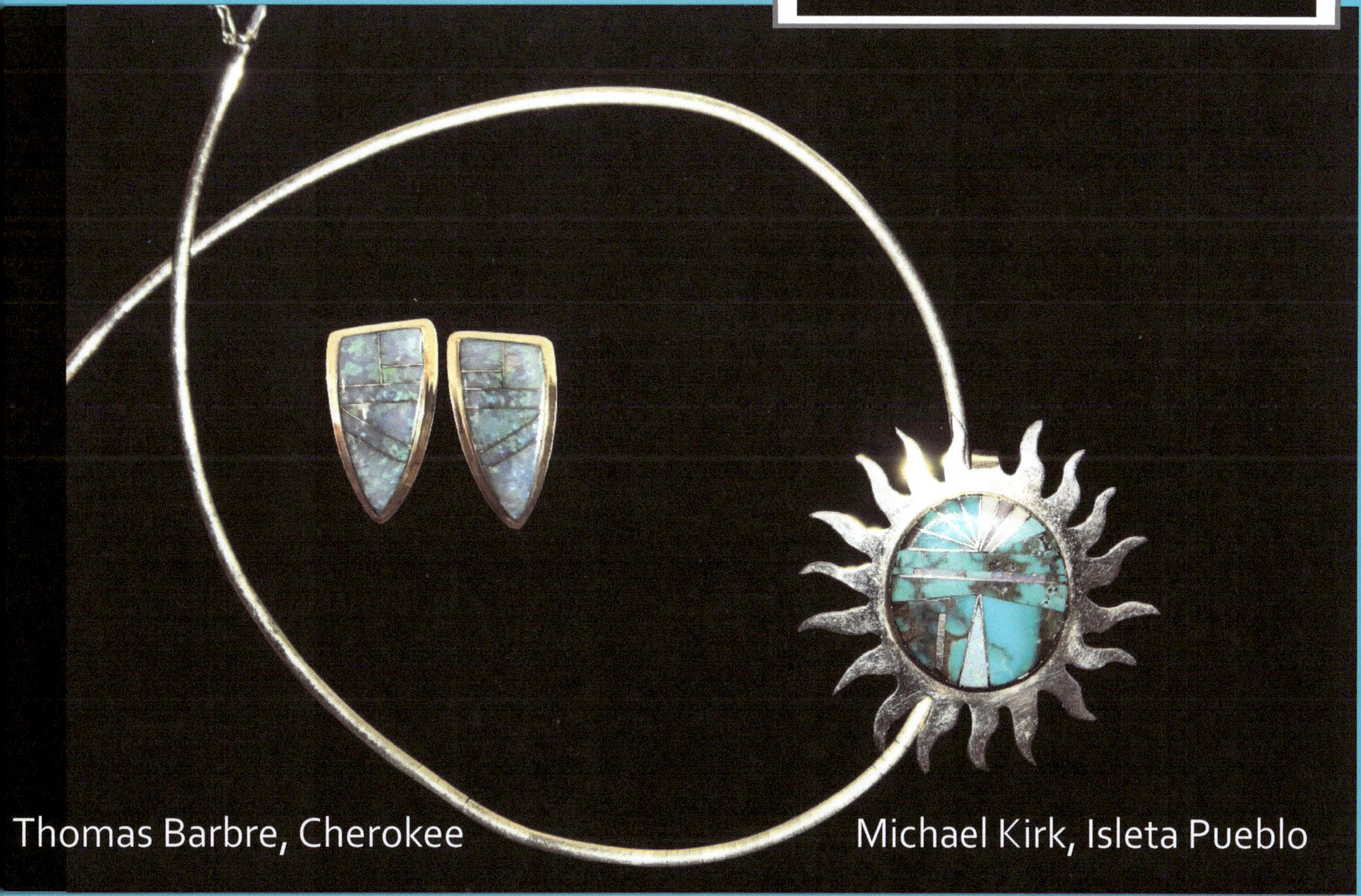

Thomas Barbre, Cherokee

Michael Kirk, Isleta Pueblo

Lapis Lazuli

The deep, rich blue of lapis lazuli makes it a favored counterpoint to the lighter colors of the turquoise stone. These stones have been mined since ancient times, and exported around the world from their original mines in Afghanistan. Today lapis mines exist in many countries, including Russia, Canada, Chile, and the United States.

Lapis is a harder stone, and takes a very nice shine when polished. The highest quality stones have a blue to purplish-blue hue and an even color. Lapis Lazuli is also ground into fine dust and made into a paint pigment that results in the color of ultramarine.

The deep blue of lapis seems to pop when accent colors are added. Here both artist have enhanced the lapis with the accents of sterling silver, Onyx, Tigers Eye, Spiny Oyster, Gold and Silver overlay beads.

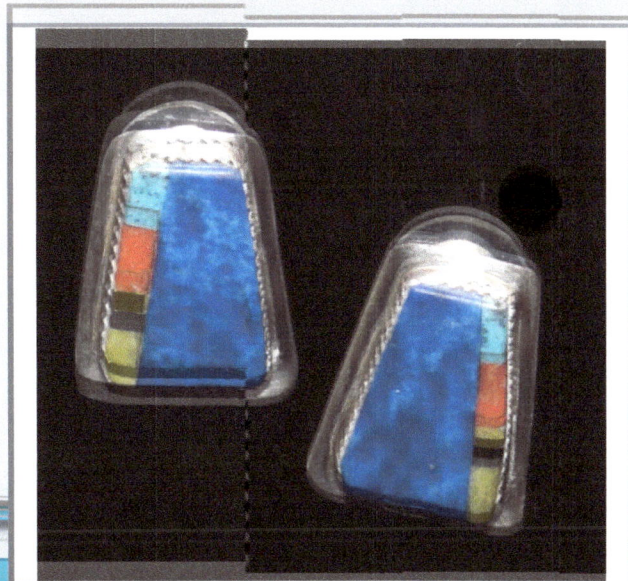

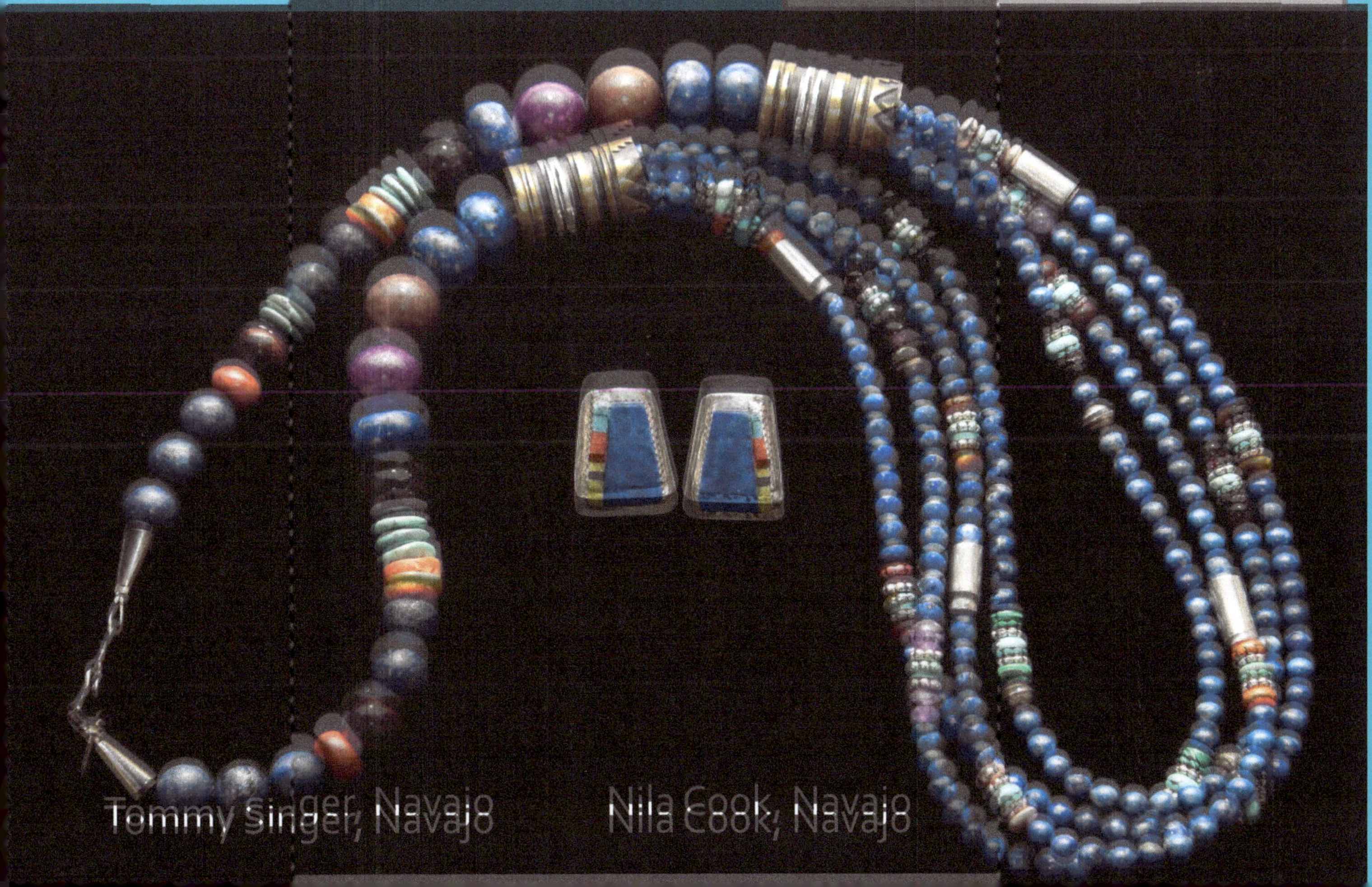

Tommy Singer, Navajo   Nila Cook, Navajo

Albert and Ken allow the high quality of the stones to shine in this statement ring and cuff. The marvelous deep dark blue of the natural lapis is enhanced only by the sparkle of the highly polished sterling silver.

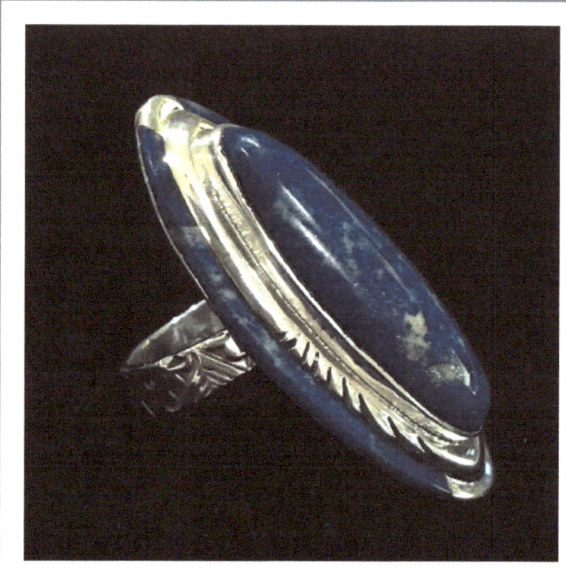

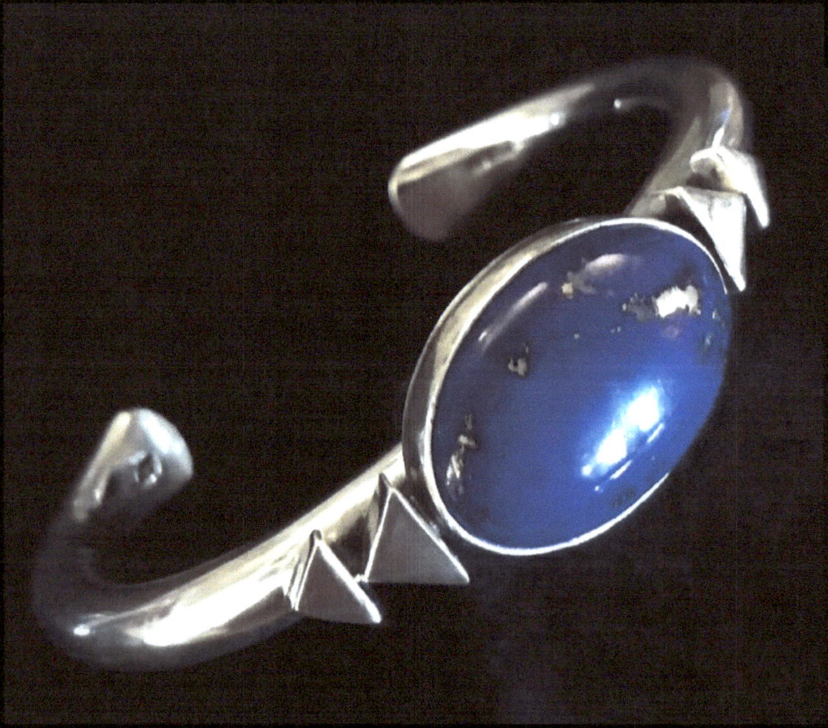

Albert Lee, Navajo

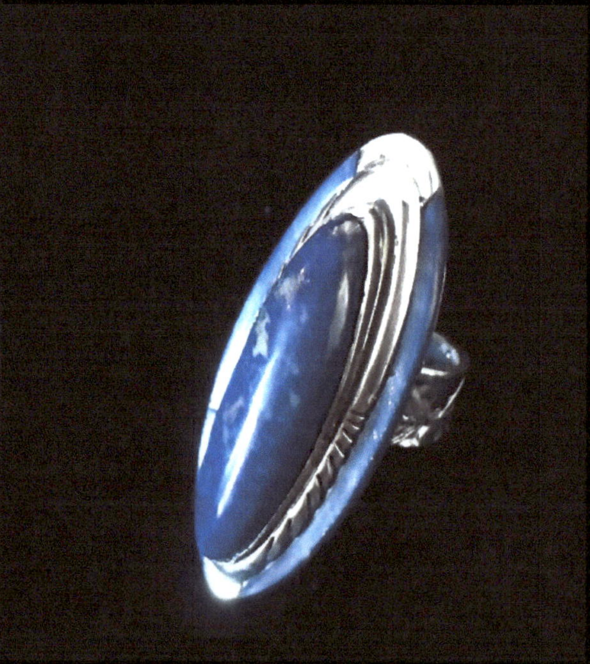

Ken Romero, Taos Pueblo

Channel inlaid stones of turquoise, lapis and sugilite bring harmony to this contemporary cuff. The accents of the sterling silver native designs on either side of the cuff add to the uniqueness of the design.

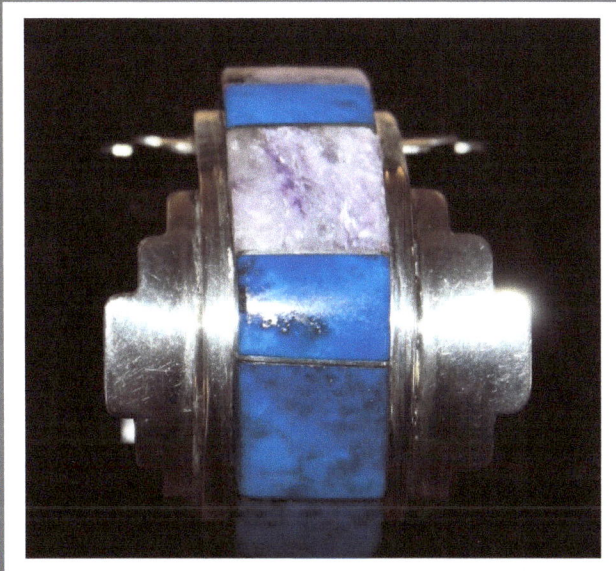

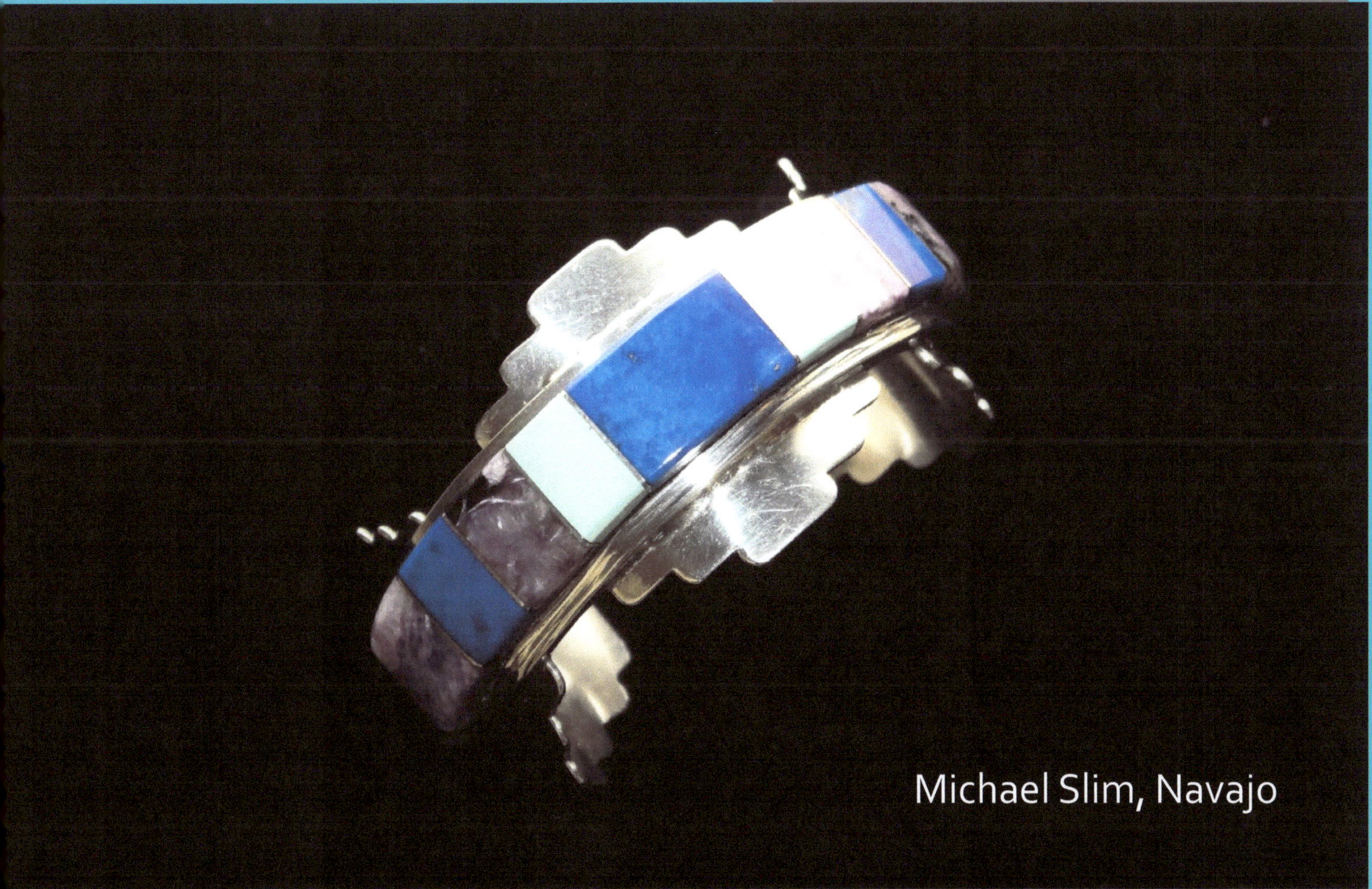

Michael Slim, Navajo

Pearls

The origin of pearls is simple – the mollusk has an irritation, and forms a secretion around it – thus, the pearl is formed.

Most pearls are irregular and discolored, but there are some that are spherical and perfectly white. These are what are most commonly found on the elegant strands of dress pearls.

However, the very rare, highly prized Tahitian Black Pearl is finding its way into Native American jewelry. These pearls come only from the black lip oyster around the waters of Tahiti, and are very versatile in jewelry settings.

Exquisite Tahitian pearls adorn the tiny flowers on these unique cuttlefish bone cast pieces. The cuttlefish, the dragonflies, and the pearls are all water symbols, emphasizing the importance of water in the arid Southwest.

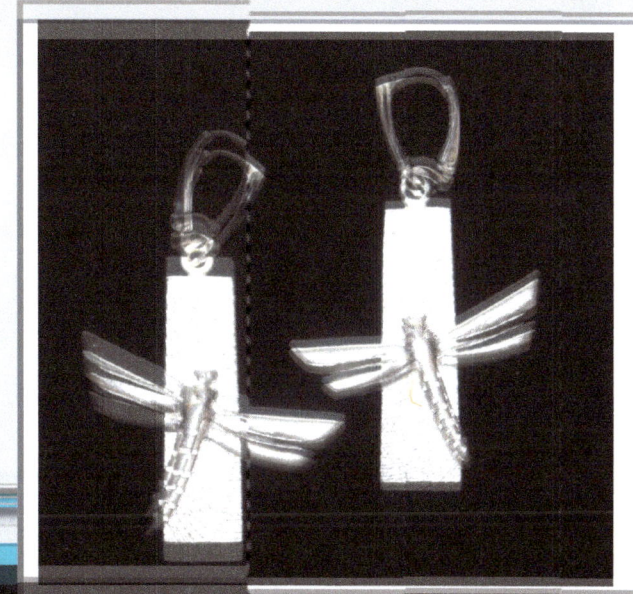

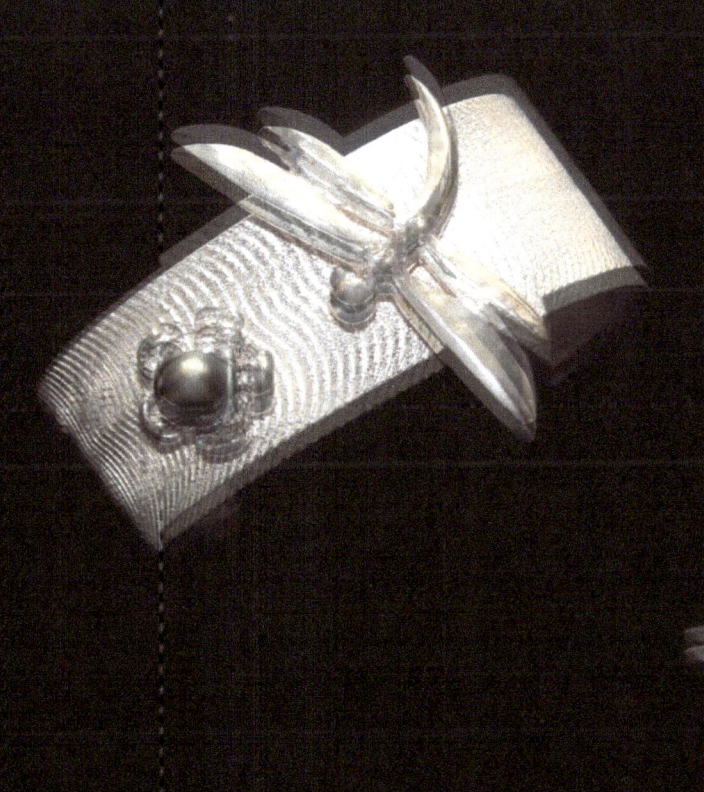

Althea Cajero, Acoma Pueblo

Coral
Adding a New Perspective

Top jewelers will tell you that the best coral comes from the deep waters of the Mediterranean. The deeper the water, the more rich and vibrant the deep red color becomes.

Unfortunately, the demand for deep water Mediterranean coral has resulted in a dramatically depleted supply, and this has resulted in dyed substitutes being sold in the market as true coral.

Unlike most gemstones, coral is actually the external skeleton of the coral polyp, a marine invertebrate. The Great Barrier Reef in Australia is an example of a large coral colony.

The cuttlefish bone design forms the backdrop, while the deep red Mediterranean coral cabochon provides a dramatic juxtaposition to the shiny sterling silver band floating above the cuff. The deep red coral in the earrings is enhanced with 18k gold swirls.

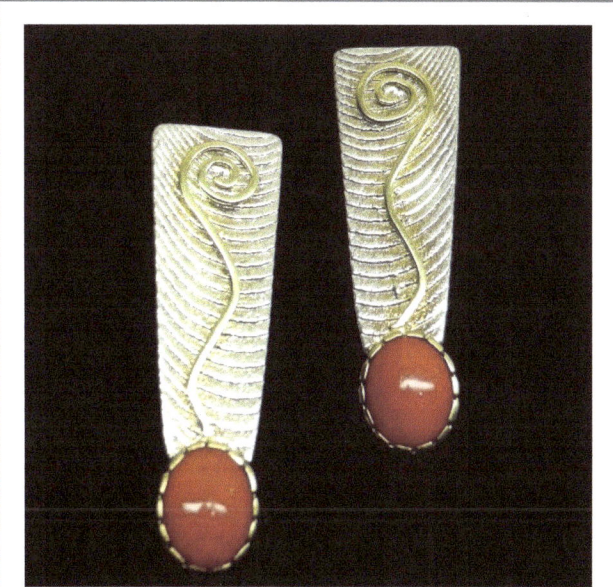

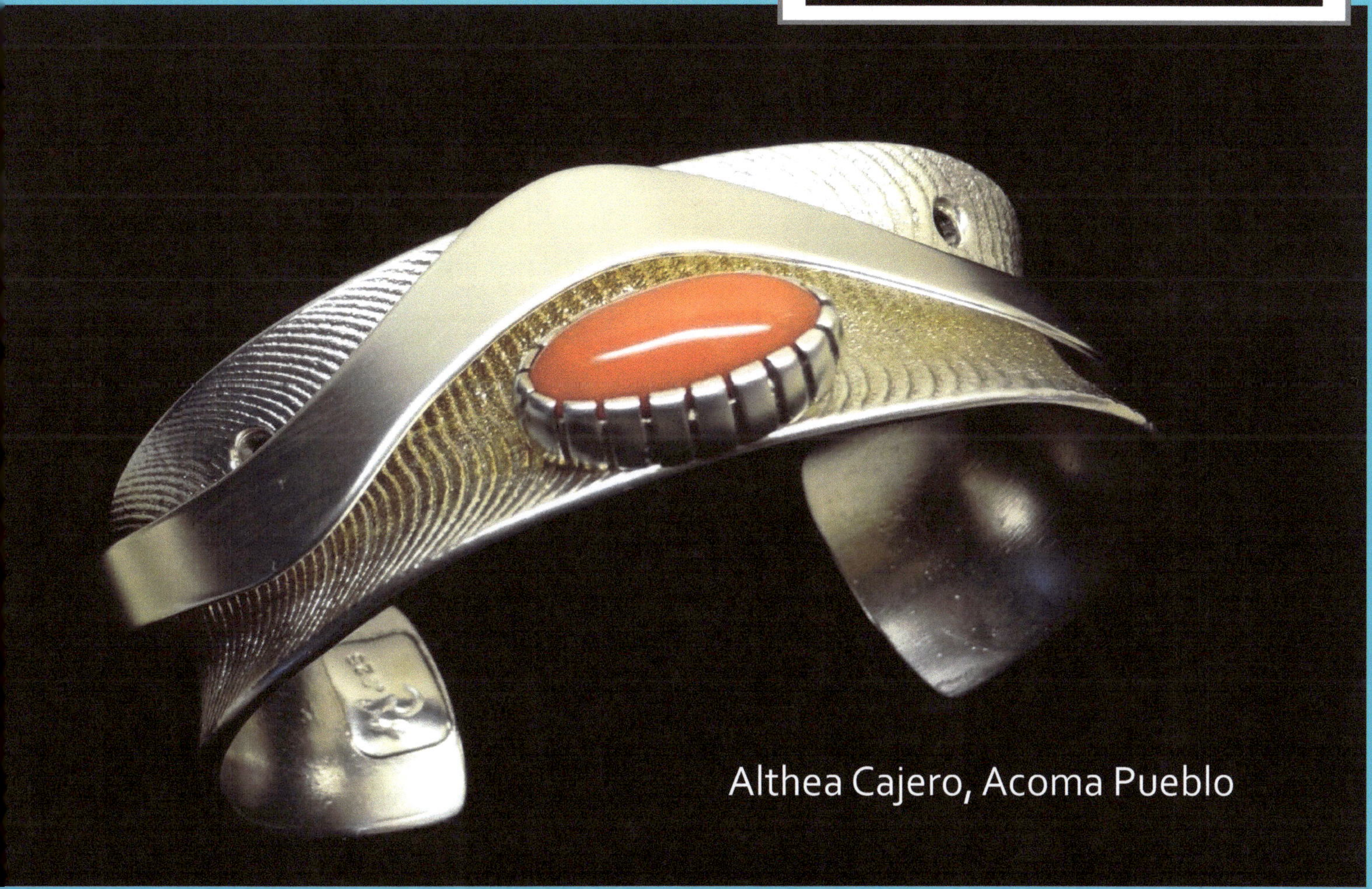

Althea Cajero, Acoma Pueblo

Spiny Oyster

The spiny oyster is misnamed, as it really isn't an oyster. They actually fall in the same family as scallops. The spiny oyster is also known as spondylus.

Spiny oysters have been harvested for food for the past 15,000 years or so, and the hard, decorative exterior shells rapidly became favored as both jewelry and currency.

The spiny oyster has a wonderful, vibrant orange color that looks fantastic on its own or paired with other gemstones. Tommy Jackson and Albert Lee have expertly cut, ground, and polished the spiny oyster to showcase the beautiful deep orange-red colors.

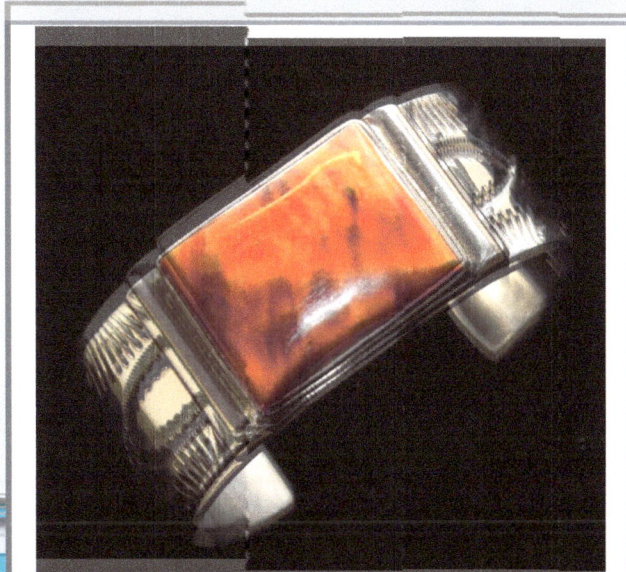

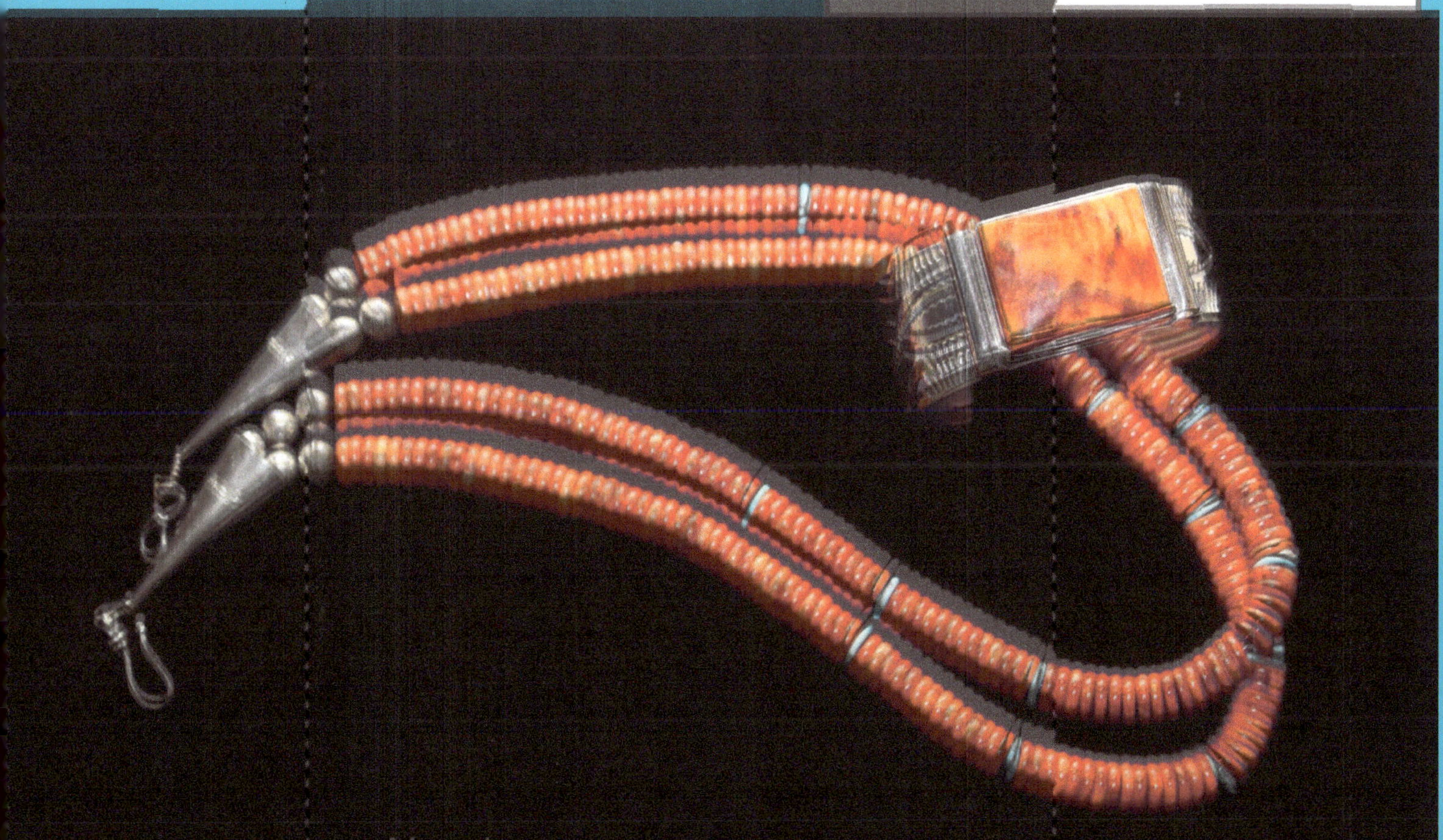

Tommy Jackson, Navajo

Albert Lee, Navajo

Unique Designs

A number of talented jewelers are developing unique designs for their works, incorporating many traditional design elements with more contemporary presentations.

Each artist strives to blend the traditional motifs and patterns of their culture with a new, innovative look. They are telling a story of the evolution of their cultures with their art, in addition to creating stunning jewelry.

Unlike traditional Native American jewelry, these unique designs fit into almost any ensemble or style, and are not identified as solely Native American in style.

This stunning and unique sterling silver cuff is designed in shape of an arrow, which is inlaid with turquoise and coral. The end of the arrow is adorned with a dangling feather, also inlaid with turquoise and coral. This magnificent bracelet is both traditional and innovative at the same time.

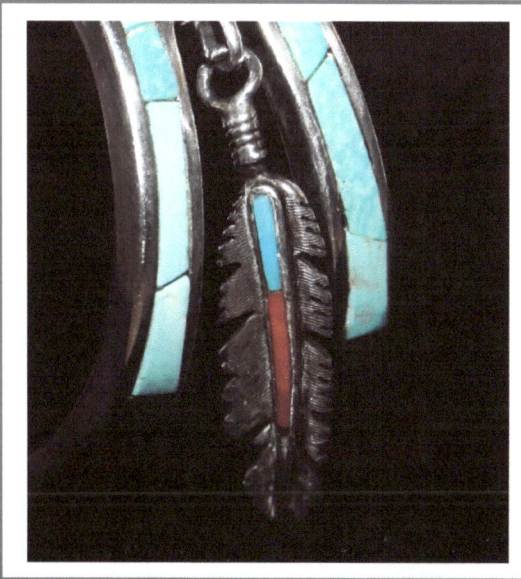

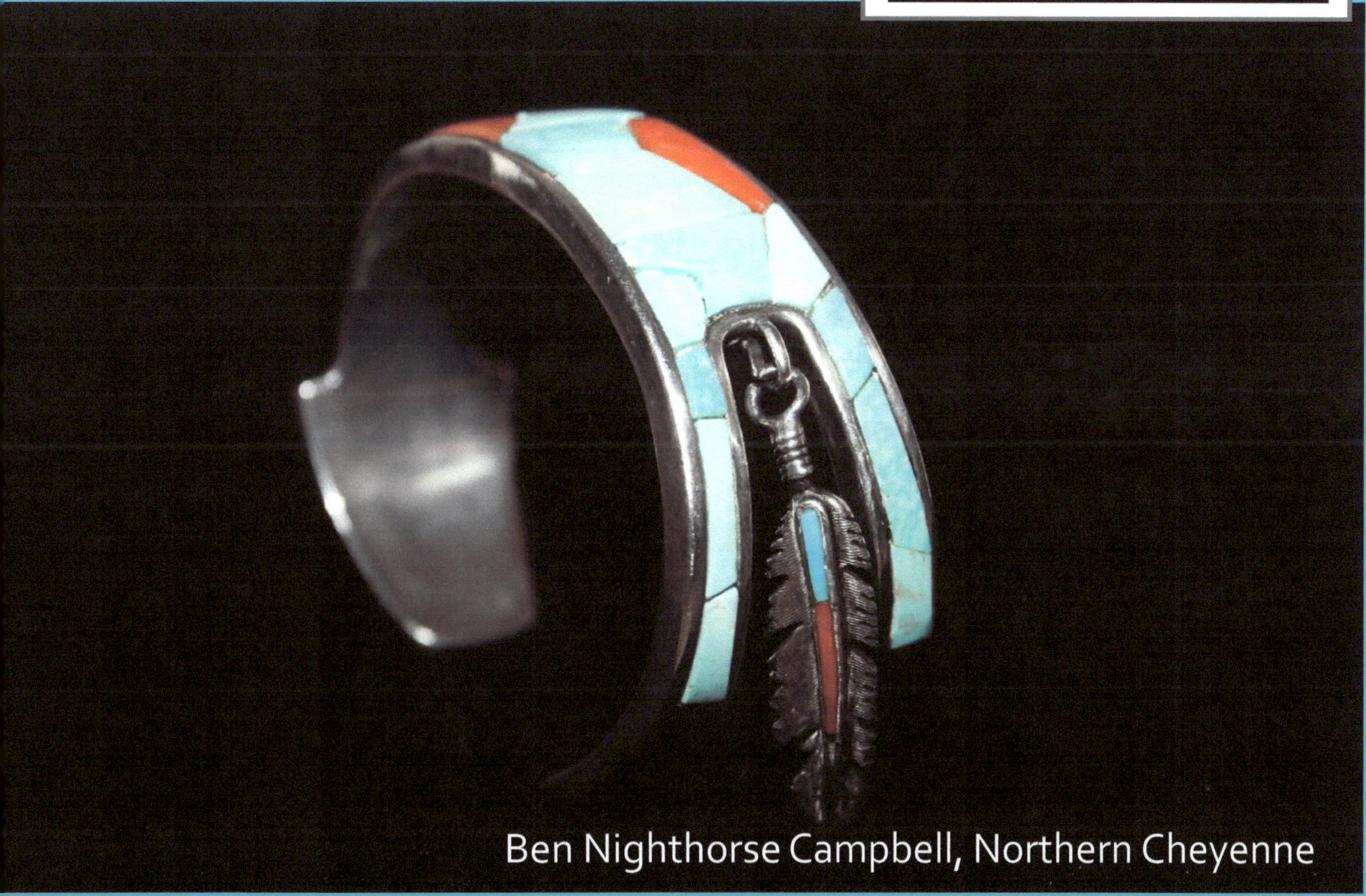

Ben Nighthorse Campbell, Northern Cheyenne

This unique roll milled cuff of sterling silver flows with swirls and circles both on the top and the underside. It is topped with Althea's signature sterling silver dragonfly. The swirls and circles ever reminiscent of the importance of water.

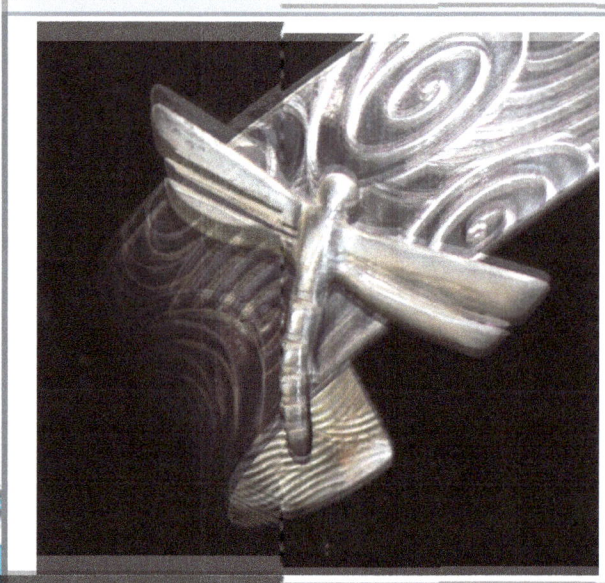

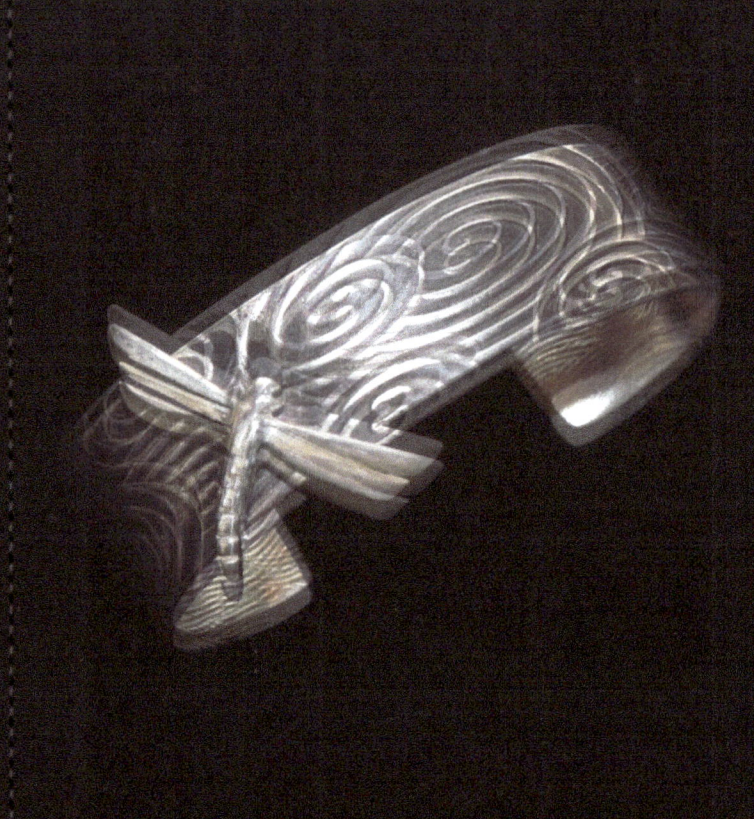

Althea Cajero, Acoma Pueblo

Jan Loco prefers the unusual look of individual rock formations to enhance and texture of her jewelry. She pours the molten sterling silver onto a rock and hammers it to achieve unique designs. This rock hammered sterling silver turtle can be a pin or a pendant.

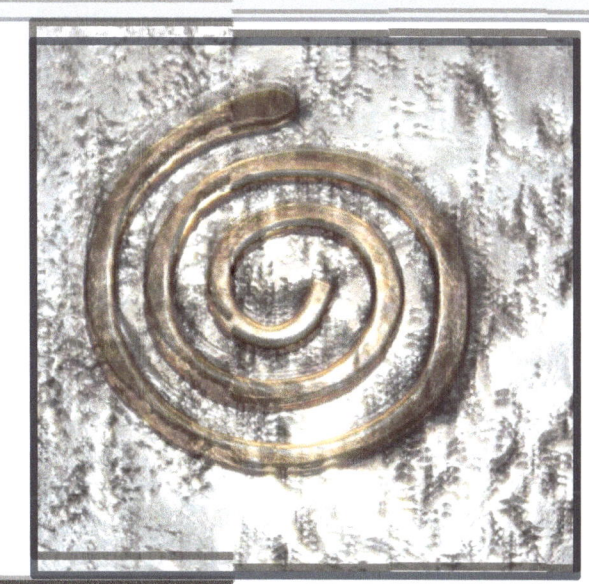

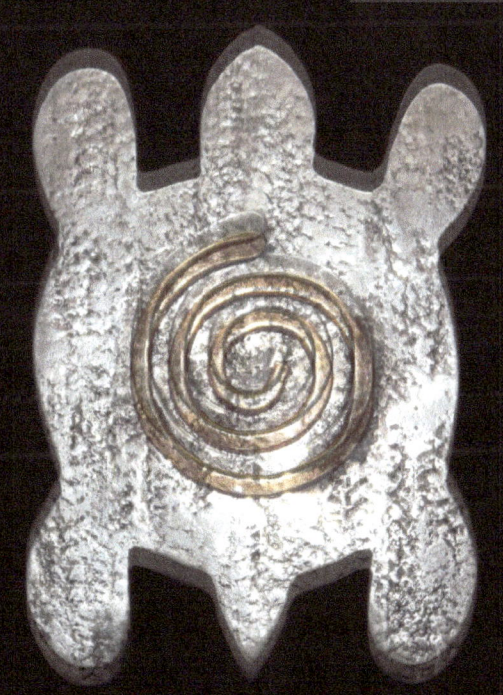

Jan Loco, Warm Springs Apache

Micro Inlay

A traditional approach to fastening gemstones to a base material is the use of a bezel. The bezel prongs hold the gemstones in place for display. A newer technique is the use of channel inlay, in which the jewelers lay precisely cut gemstones into premade silver channels. This technique is particularly favored by Native American artists of the American Southwest.

An even newer and more difficult technique is that of micro-inlay. The gemstones are cut in very thin, precise slices and stacked together, often to create a picture or tell a story. This technique takes very steady hands and nerves of steel.

Micro inlay techniques illustrate how dynamic and fabulous Navajo jewelry can be. This beautiful necklace took many tedious hours to create using the smallest of natural stones and sterling silver. Abraham created the beads to match the sterling silver inlay design on the pendant.

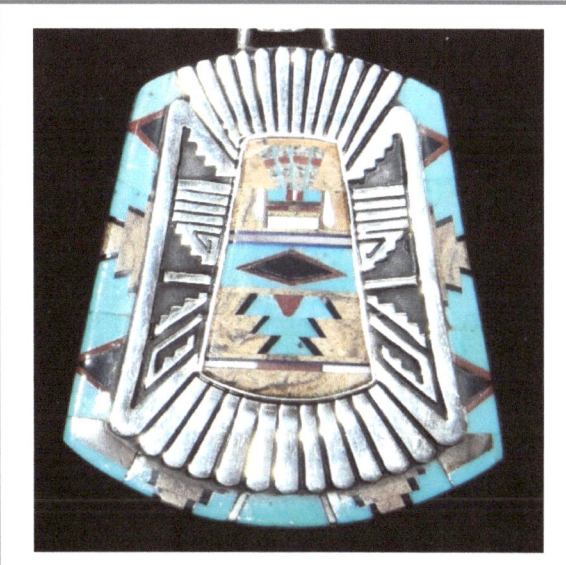

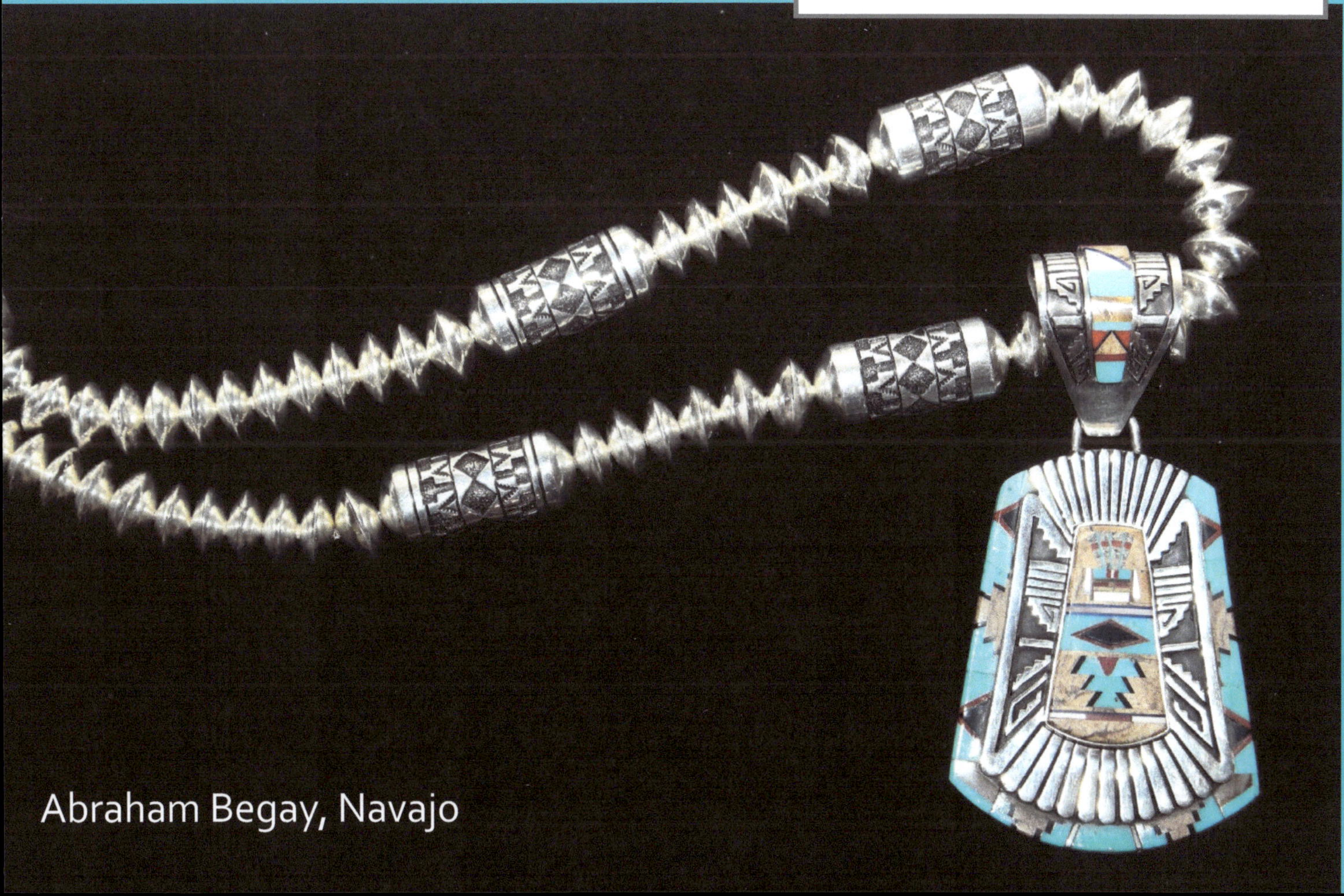

Abraham Begay, Navajo

This trapezoidal bolo features intricate micro-inlay of beautiful turquoise, jet, mother-of-pearl and pen shell. These gemstones balance perfectly with the top layer of sterling silver and carved inlaid gemstones. The center of the pendant is flanked with sterling silver panels carved with water symbols.

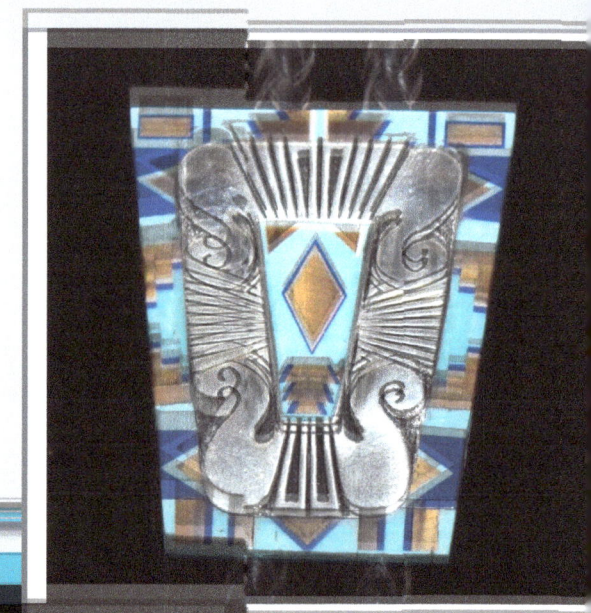

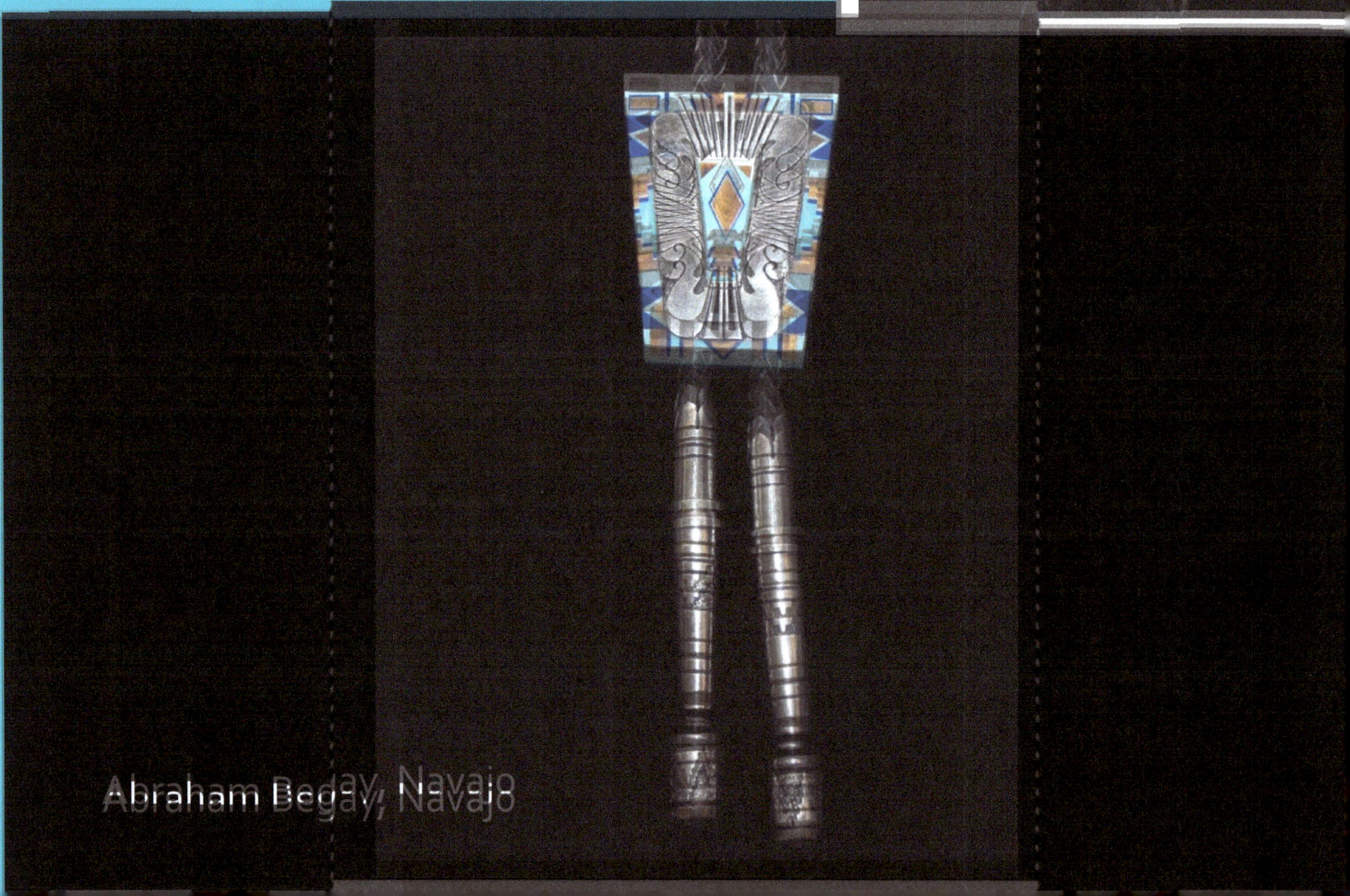

Abraham Begay, Navajo

Stone to stone inlay requires a great deal of skill and very steady hands. The intricate and delicate designs in the jewelry of Abraham Begay and Alvin Yellowhorse exemplify their mastery of this technique in these pieces.

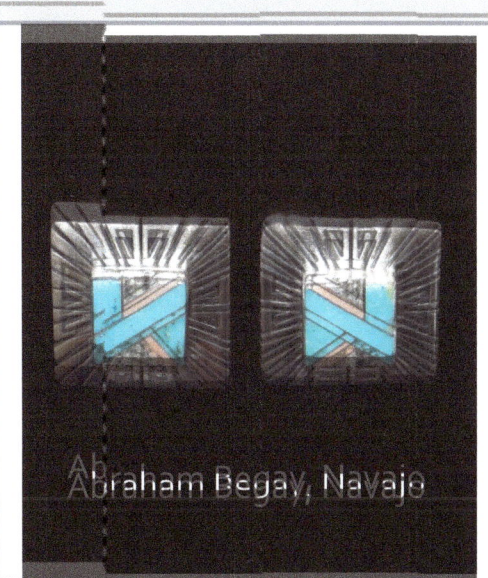

Abraham Begay, Navajo

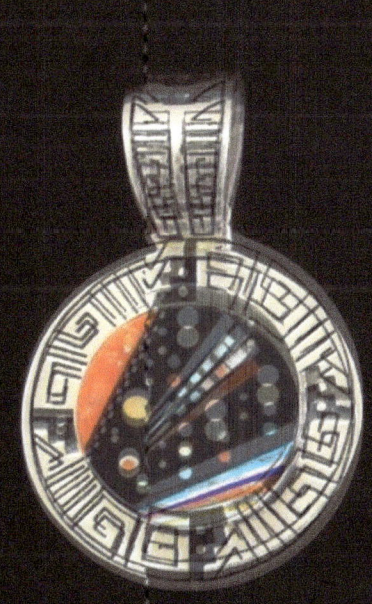

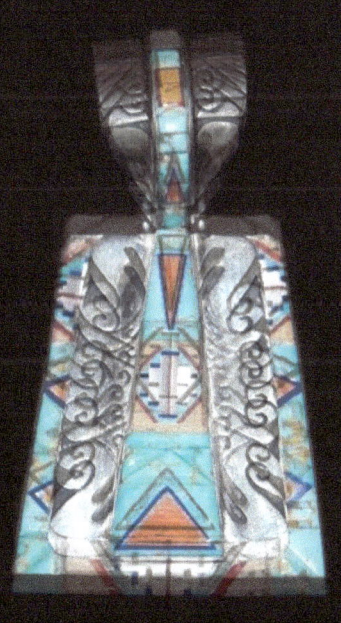

Abraham Begay, Navajo

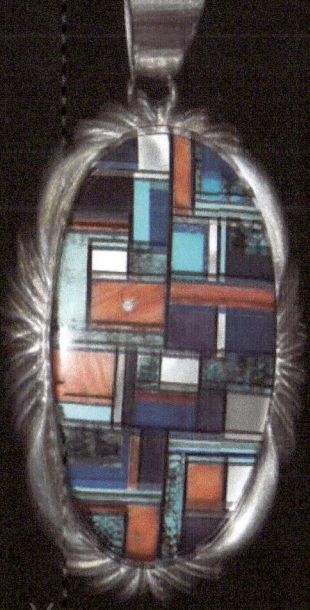

Alvin Yellowhorse, Navajo

Cobblestone and Corn Row

Similar to a cobblestone road, where the pavement consists of individual stones that may or may not be particularly even, cobblestone inlay is a technique where gemstones are cut and set into the bezel or channel.

The surfaces of the stones are not flat across, creating interesting dimension and contrasts of the different gemstones utilized. Often, the stones are fitted at angles to each other, similar to a courtyard stone pattern.

A similar inlay pattern called cornrow has the stone pieces all laid in parallel, like corn kernels on a cob. The edges of each stone is usually rounded.

The uniqueness of cobblestone and corn row inlay designs require the artists to shape each stone and individually set them in a pattern between tiny pieces of silver. Steve, Alvin and Ken are masters at the delicate art of cutting of stones to create these inlaid patterns.

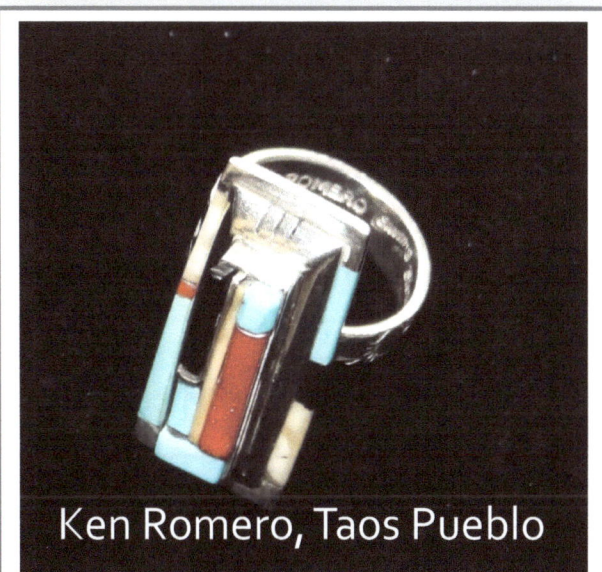

Ken Romero, Taos Pueblo

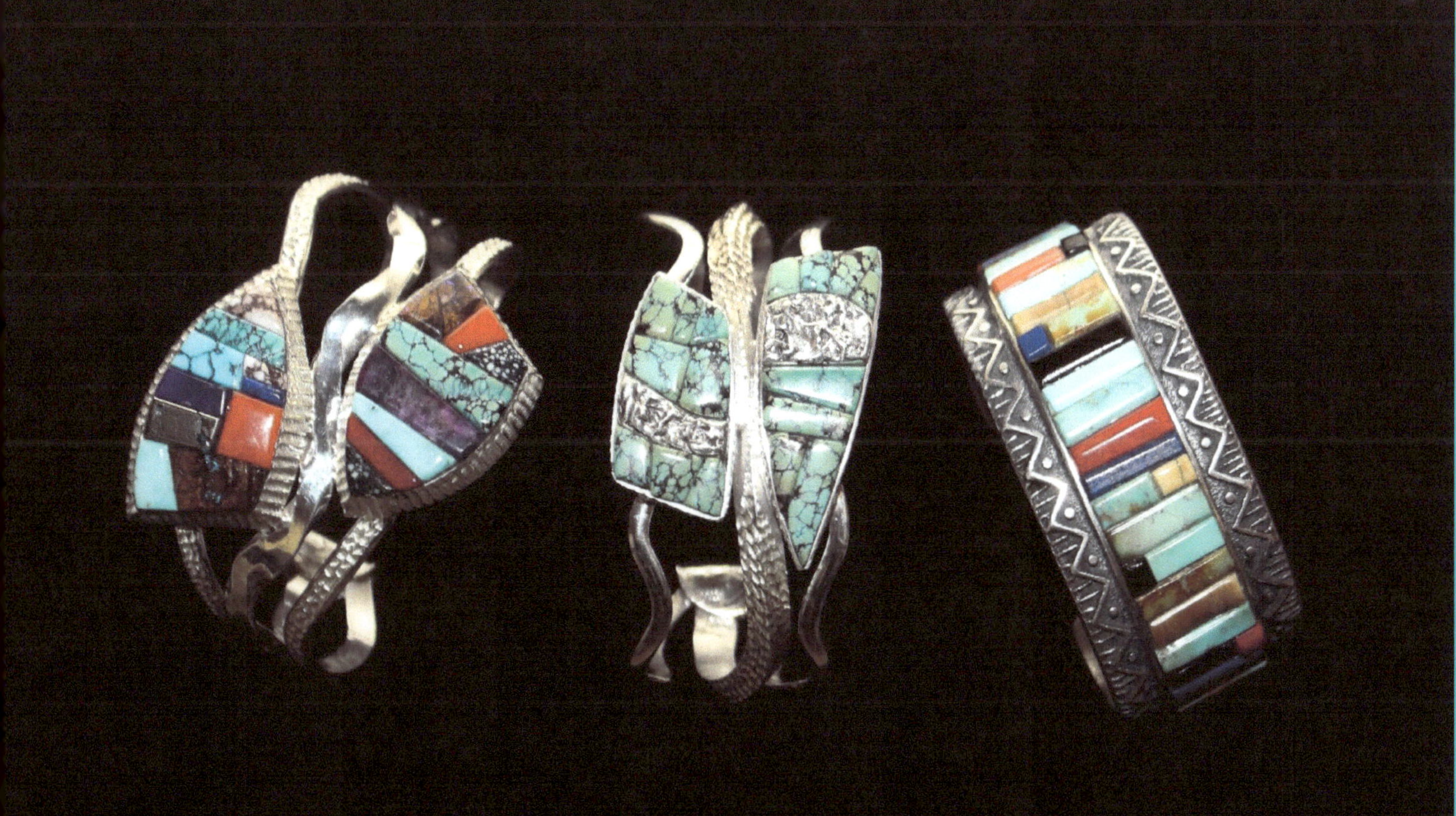

Alvin Yellowhorse, Navajo

Steve LaRance, Hopi

Tufa Cast

Someone once said, "What is old is new again." The technique of tufa casting is not new, but it is extremely time consuming and delicate work.

The artist begins with two lava (tufa) stones. The stones form the opposite sides of the mold. The stones are carved into the shape and pattern desired by the artist, and then bound together. The molten silver is poured into the mold and allowed to cool. When cooled, the mold is separated and the casting is removed. The artist then polishes the portions of the casting that should be polished, and leaves the rough tufa impression on the remainder.

Each tufa mold commonly makes only a single piece of jewelry. While requiring great skill and precision, tufa stone allows an artist to be a little more creative. Here Erik and Marlin have enhanced their tufa designs with beautiful stones.

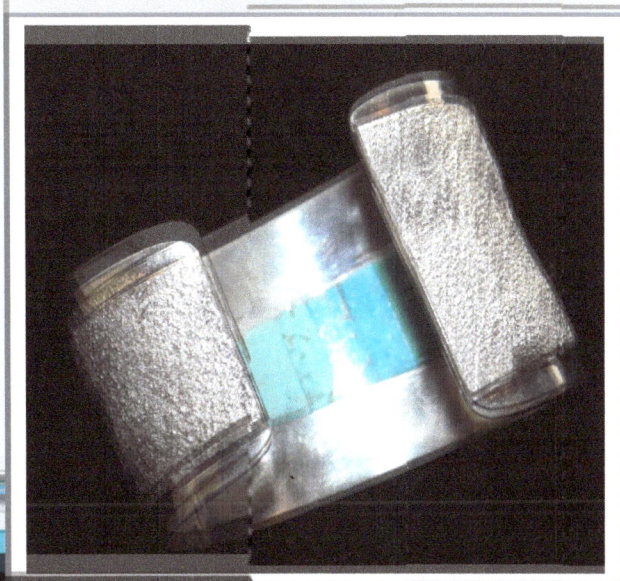

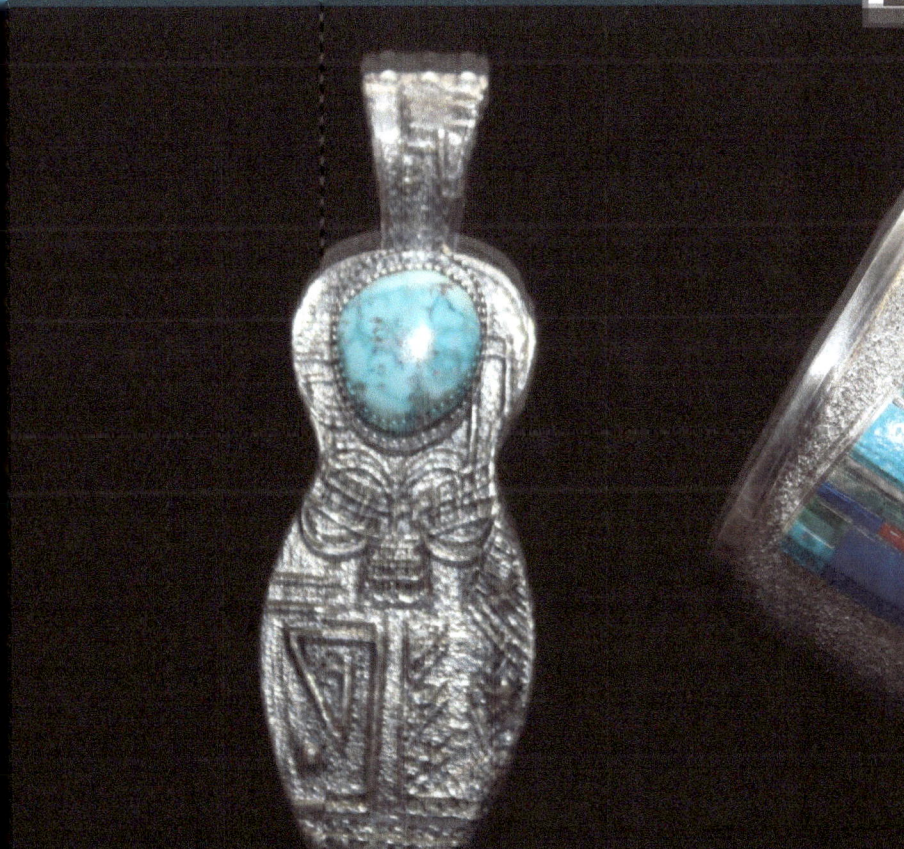

Erik Fender, San Ildefonso Pueblo

Marlin Honhongva, Hopi

The Dancing Rabbit Gallery

AUTHENTIC NATIVE AMERICAN ART

Come Explore

Online...

thedancingrabbitgallery.com

817-337-8576

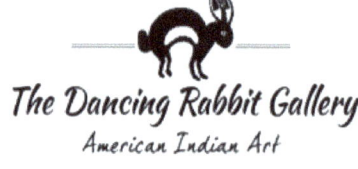

The Dancing Rabbit Gallery
American Indian Art

Founded in 1980   Online since 2012

www.ingramcontent.com/pod-product-compliance
Lightning Source LLC
Chambersburg PA
CBHW051935210526
45473CB00006B/2255